# The View...
# Our Place

# The View from Our Place

## The Australian winemaker's inside track to enjoying Australian wine

POCKET
BOOKS

LONDON • SYDNEY • NEW YORK • TORONTO

First published in Great Britain by Simon & Schuster UK Ltd, 2006
First published by Pocket Books, 2006
An imprint of Simon & Schuster UK Ltd
A CBS COMPANY

1 3 5 7 9 10 8 6 4 2

Simon & Schuster UK Ltd, Africa House, 64-78 Kingsway, London WC2B 6AH

www.simonsays.co.uk

Simon & Schuster Australia, Sydney

A CIP catalogue record for this book is available from the British Library

ISBN 1416526811

Designed by Andy Summers, Planet Creative
Edited by Richard Williams

Thanks to Chris Shanahan for his help with this project.

Printed in China

# Contents

# Foreword

I've been working with Australian wines for over 40 years, of which the last 15 have been spent travelling the world talking and answering questions about wine. During this time I've always been surprised by how few people know that Jacob's Creek is a real place, and how little they know about what goes on here. People tell me that they want to learn more about our wines but not get bogged down with technical details or feel challenged about their understanding and knowledge. They like to hear interesting facts, tips and hints, and honest opinions. So after years of telling it like it is, face-to-face, it seemed a good idea to put it all down in writing.

I hope you enjoy reading about Australian wines in general, and Jacob's Creek in particular. I am sure that knowing a bit more about wine will increase your pleasure next time you raise a glass to your lips.

*Philip Laffer*

# Australian Wine

When it comes to Australian wine, words like freshness, generosity, flavour, softness and roundness come to mind. These are the characteristics that make our wines easy and pleasant to drink and the reason why they're so popular around the world.

They taste as they do for a lot of reasons. We use the right grape varieties. We enjoy a warm climate that's ideal for ripening grapes.

Our early pioneers brought with them grape varieties from European regions that have significantly cooler climates than Australia — one of the oldest, driest and warmest continents earth. Our winemakers had to learn to deal with grapes which, while very ripe and flavoursome tended to be naturally low in acid — and therefore more prone to degradation than the higher acid grapes handled by winemakers in cooler European regions. Similarly, making wine in hot weather presented challenges — particularly in controlling the fermentation process.

In this fragile situation Australian winemakers learned to be particularly careful. Had they not, they could only ever have made pretty ordinary wine.

Australians really started drinking wine in a serious way with the advent in the 1950s and 1960s of products with wonderful names such as Rhinegold, Barossa Pearl and Ben Ean Moselle. These are now as unfashionable as the sweet German hock that was popular in the UK market in the 1960s.

## Great winemaking in search of flavour

They were all white wines, they were all sweet and they were all well made. At the time, the grape variety didn't matter much. They were fresh, balanced wines. Each was attractive to drink and, collectively, this style persuaded Australians into drinking wine. So we had a quite different background to other parts of the world where many people started drinking pretty ordinary wine.

Then along came wine-boxes in the 1970s — and the same thing happened. While generic, and you might say bland, they were well-made, good-quality wines. I suppose that's one of the reasons why bag-in-the-box has never had the same poor image in Australia as it has elsewhere.

*A typical Australian vineyard: Jacob's Creek in the Barossa Valley.*

## The right grape varieties

Then as we started moving increasingly into varietal winemaking, we began dealing with better-quality fruit — and good winemaking brought out the distinctive characters of each grape variety. This meant that we were able to offer Australian wine drinkers good wine at prices they could afford. That soon moved Australians from sweet, generic white wines on to dry, varietal table wines.

It was when we began exporting the kinds of wine being enjoyed in Australia that our wines took off internationally. One of the reasons they succeeded, I think, is because a lot of wine consumed in Australia and in the UK is a social drink, rather than drunk with meals. A lot of European styles are quite difficult in that situation. The reds tend to be fairly astringent and the whites leaner and more austere than Australian styles.

## Fresher, fruitier flavours

In contrast, Australian wines are generous — in the sense that they've got plenty of alcohol, the fruit's ripe, so there aren't any green or weedy flavours, and the wines are well made — so you tend to get fresher, fruitier flavours than you do in similarly priced European wines. Furthermore, the next bottle you buy is going to be very similar, because Australian wines have a high level of reliability — and that goes back to the culture of attentive winemaking.

## A high batting average

I think that in Australia we have a higher average wine quality than anywhere else in the world because we don't have a bad bottom end. Even our cheapest commercial wines are well made and appealing.

This is because we don't have different winemakers for different ends of the market. For example, the people who make Penfolds Grange are the same people who make Penfolds Rawson's Retreat. Here at Jacob's Creek, the person making £30-a-bottle Johann Shiraz Cabernet is the same person responsible for making £5-a-bottle Jacob's Creek Shiraz Cabernet.

> *Australian wines have a high level of reliability*

## Diverse soils and climates

That doesn't mean, though, that we make homogenous wines – far from it. The sheer diversity of grape varieties, soils and climates guarantees a wide range of flavours and styles. Although it's easy from a distance to think of Australia as one big, hot country, it's actually amazingly varied. In the eastern states, source of the majority of our wine, vineyards are scattered over 1000km from north to south – greater than the distance from London to Inverness. And it's over 3000km from our easternmost to our westernmost vineyards – think of London to Cairo!

With vineyards planted from near sea level to 1000m above it, on every imaginable aspect, on endlessly variable soils, and in coastal as well as continental locations, it's not surprising that Australia's 2000 winemakers should offer such a wide spectrum of wine styles.

## Think Shiraz, think Australia

Within that spectrum we have a few specialities, notably Shiraz and Riesling. We've adopted Shiraz as our own because we're one of the few countries that makes it really well. Australia doesn't make Riesling in great volume but it has a great reputation. It goes back to when Australia was locked down in quarantine in the 1880s because of phylloxera (the vine louse that decimated European vineyards in the late 19th century). The significant white varieties that existed in Australia then were Semillon, Riesling and Crouchen.

So when we started drinking quality table wines in the 1950s, 60s and 70s, they were made from Semillon and Riesling. Traditionally these varieties are not oak matured — because it doesn't suit them. Therefore we learned to make wines that had great longevity because they were not early developers that had been forced along in barrels.

So we focused on making these two very classic wines. Now, for Riesling to taste like Riesling, it has to have cool nights. So it became concentrated in the cooler Eden Valley, Clare Valley and the slopes of the Barossa.

## Good Riesling vineyards

We were lucky as an industry that we didn't lose all those Riesling vineyards when the Chardonnay boom began in the 1980s. Private growers pulled out nearly all of their Riesling — they just couldn't get the price for the fruit. But proprietary winemakers such as Orlando, Lindemans, Leo Burings, Hardys, Yalumba, and Penfolds in particular, hung on to their Riesling vines.

We are as a company, and as an industry, surrounded by remarkably good Riesling vineyards. And in Australia we have a history of making very good, long-lived Riesling. With the superb fruit that we have, that's just a case of being very careful all the way from the vine through to the bottle.

*The first Shiraz vines arrived in Australia in the 1830s. They flourished in the warm weather and thin soils, and were used to make fortified wines by maturing in oak barrels such as these.*

# Our Place

Jacob's Creek is our place. It's where our story began in 1847 when Johann Gramp planted vines. It's still our home today -- visited each year by thousands of wine tourists.

It's in the Barossa Valley, about 80km north of Adelaide, the capital of the State of South Australia. We're about 1400km west of Sydney and 800km northwest of Melbourne. Apart from Adelaide there aren't too many landmarks that might be familiar to overseas visitors. The Barossa itself is probably the biggest and most recognised attraction.

To imagine where Jacob's Creek is, think of the Barossa as being shaped like a funnel. We're at the southern end where the floor of the valley is about 500m wide. If you continue on to the northern end, up around Ebenezer, about 20km due north, it's about 10km wide.

*Johann Gramp – wine pioneer*

So it opens right out in the north, where it's flatter and, because it's more elevated, the hills forming the eastern boundary seem lower. At our end of the valley the country's more undulating, the valley's narrower, and the eastern Barossa Ranges and slopes dominate our environment. Jacob's Creek itself flows down from these hills before emptying into the North Para River.

## Our story

The Jacob's Creek vineyard lies on the valley floor and slopes on the eastern side of the creek in the vicinity of Johann Gramp's original winery and family home, both now beautifully restored. This is where our story began.

Johannes Menge was a geologist-cum-botanist, employed by the South Australian Company to look around parts of South Australia. He based himself at Jacob's Creek. Being as much interested in agriculture and botany as he was in geology, he established pilot plantings of many things, including vines. On his return to Adelaide, he reported that there was a wonderful place in the Barossa where you could grow all sorts of things.

Jacob's Creek had originally been named when Colonel William Light, the surveyor of South Australia, surveyed the Barossa. One of his colleagues was William Jacob, an assistant surveyor. Jacob apparently convinced Light to name this little creek after him, so there'd be some recognition for his family as time went on.

There must be more to it than that, because shortly afterwards, Jacob retired from surveying and bought a property on Jacob's Creek — at the very spot where Menge had conducted his experimental plantings.

"*Making wine soon became Johann Gramp's real purpose in life*"

*Jacob's Creek - the river itself.*

## Jacob and Johann

Menge had lived in a cave, and when Gramp and Jacob began building houses and wineries, that's where they got the stone. What used to be a cave is now a depression – and a South Australian historic site.

So Jacob lived here on Jacob's Creek as a neighbour to Johann Gramp. The ruins of Jacob's original house still exist. His subsequent house remains in reasonably good repair. In fact, guests of Jacob's Creek stay there when they're visiting us.

## The Barossa Valley's first commercial vineyard

Vines already existed in the Barossa Valley when Johann Gramp arrived with a number of other German immigrants in the 1840s. But there were only three or four rows of vines – and these were devoted to making sacramental wine for the Lutheran Church.

Gramp established what we believe was a general farm on Jacob's Creek. As part of this, in 1847, he planted the Barossa Valley's first commercial vineyard – a few acres of Riesling. While grape growing and making wine was originally only a part of his farming activity, it soon became Johann Gramp's real purpose in life.

The fact that Riesling came first may, in part, explain our fascination for this variety across our entire history. In that time we've learned a lot about how to grow it and make tremendously appealing white wines from it.

Riesling remains one of our key varieties. We still grow it at Jacob's Creek and we grow nothing but Riesling on Steingarten Vineyard, higher up on the catchment. It's fascinating to think that after 160 years we still source some of our finest Riesling within sight of Johann Gramp's original vineyard.

# Our People

For those of us who make Jacob's Creek, it's our passion, our life, our challenge and our pleasure. I don't think I've ever woken up and said, I don't want to go work. I routinely get up early and aim to be at work by 7.00 or 7.30 a.m. — and I might drop in at a vineyard or two on the way.

One of my challenges here is to ensure that we have the right people for winemaking and viticulture. The people we look for are first and foremost passionate about wine. They must be able to discriminate between wines and have performed well academically.

## Getting things right

We've got about 20 winemakers and they're the sort of people who are concerned with getting things right. For example, a winemaker might prepare a blend in five minutes. Or he or she could say, look I want to try this, that or the other — and might stay there for five hours before being satisfied.

That's the Jacob's Creek approach. Even if we ended up where we'd started, we'd be satisfied that we'd tried every possibility as to how to make the blend more appealing.

## Strong links all along the chain

A step back from the makers there's a group of people — viticulturists, vineyard managers, vineyard workers, people working in bottling, and grower liaison officers — who take decisions that have a significant bearing on wine quality.

Independent grape growers, too, are absolutely integral to Jacob's Creek. They have a relationship with a particular winemaker who looks after their region. There'll be a grower liaison officer as the commercial contact, and there'll be a viticulturist. So they've got three points of contact. They'll see the winemaker two or three times each year, the viticulturist half a dozen times, and the grower liaison officer almost constantly.

## Not just grape growers, but wine growers

They will also taste our wines to give them an understanding of what we are trying to achieve stylistically. The aim is to give the growers a feeling about the process and where they fit into it. This helps them understand how they can contribute to making a better bottle of wine.

The effect is that they develop a pride in the wine produced, and if their fruit achieves a higher grading, they're really chuffed, and they become even more committed.

Some of our grape-growing families have been with us for more than a century. Many more count the relationship in decades. And the majority have long-term contracts that protect their interests as well as the integrity of the wine.

> *"Some of our grape-growing families have been with us for more than a century"*

## Our people stick around

Stephen Couche has been the inspiration and marketing person responsible for Jacob's Creek all the way through. During that time lots of people have contributed in a marketing sense. But we've always had Steve sitting there guiding the process.

You only have to look at 30 years of bottle labels to see that, yes, there's been an evolution. But it's always been a managed evolution. There have been no radical steps that might confuse or upset our consumers.

## Continuity means reliability

From a winemaking viewpoint, we have people like Mark Tummel who was with Orlando for 40 years and was the initial winemaker for Jacob's Creek. Along the way he passed the baton to Robin Day who guided the brand for 17 years.

*Good wine begins with good grapes, and when and how they are harvested.*

Robin passed the responsibility to me in 1992/1993. I see myself very much as the custodian of Jacob's Creek during my period at the helm. I'm in the process of successfully developing very good people to take over from me — in the immediate future, Bernard Hickin, a winemaker with 30 years experience with us.

*Bernard Hickin*

## The food angle

If you're going to be a good winemaker you have to be passionate about food, too. That holds doubly true for Jacob's Creek winemakers because eight or nine out of every ten bottles of our wine are consumed with food.

That's why we also have on our team a stunningly good chef who is fascinated by wine and food matching. She has kitchens at the Jacob's Creek Visitor Centre and in the Gramp homestead. She comes up with dishes to suit our wines. So we've got the opportunity to say to our customers, here are all these recipes — some simple, some complex — that work with our wines, and here are the reasons why.

*The Jacob's Creek Visitor Centre*

# Our Heritage

The Barossa is a wonderful place to live and work. It typifies what Australia is all about. It's rural. There are little townships, the largest of 3500 people, and the smallest one of about 100. It's small and varied.

It's a spectacular place. We have cool winters around 15 degrees Celsius. We have warm summers around 30 to 40 degrees. There's open space. There are places in the Barossa where you can sit all day and not see a car.

*In summer, the hills go brown and make a striking contrast with the green vines in the valley.*

The most appealing time to me is summer, when the grass on the hills dries out and goes brown. I reckon the contrast to the green vines in the valley then is absolutely stunning.

## Jacob's Creek today

In recent years we have gone to great pains to bring Jacob's Creek itself back to the way it was when Johann Gramp established his vineyard.

We've re-planted indigenous trees and it's now pretty much the way it would have looked and would have sounded — not actually the same kookaburras and magpies, because it's a few generations on, but the bird life is still the same.

Sure, if you listen, you might hear a truck on the road or a tractor in the vineyard, but so much is identical. We still grow vines — the same varieties from the same cultivars.

The soil's the same. The climate's the same. The hills still look the same. And Jacob's Creek itself still looks as it did when Johann Gramp first planted vines here in 1847.

Gramp made wine in his original winery until he died. But he did not use the name Jacob's Creek at all. Some time after his death, the family added to their holdings by buying William Jacob's property and planting more vines.

These plantings along the Creek were always known internally as Jacob's Creek Vineyard and it was the most prominent of the family's Barossa sites. But more than a century was to pass before Jacob's Creek became a wine brand.

*The German pioneers colonised the Barossa from the 1840s onwards, running mixed farms using traditional methods and transport.*

## The place becomes a brand

With rising interest in table wines in the 1970s, Orlando — as the Gramp business was now popularly known — sought ways to create new brands and new products that might appeal to growing numbers of wine drinkers. Orlando's approach was to introduce a range of generic, but also for the first time varietal wines — Moselle, Riesling, Claret and so on — by attaching each style to one of its Barossa vineyard names: Kluge's, Jacob's Creek, Lyndale and Miamba.

That's how, in 1976, Jacob's Creek Claret — a blend of Shiraz, Cabernet Sauvignon and Malbec — became the first wine in Orlando's long history to carry the Jacob's Creek name. Kluge's, Miamba and Lyndale have since disappeared, leaving Jacob's Creek — the name at the heart of all this history — as sole survivor.

*Jacob's Creek itself — the tiny stream that gave its name to an international brand.*

*The kookaburra, an Australian symbol — and a common sight in the Barossa.*

24

# European food culture

More than any other part of Australia that I can think of, the Barossa retained its ethnic identity for a very long time. This predominantly German influence continues to give us a unique food culture.

From the time the pioneering Germans arrived here in the 1840s until the 1970s, these communities tended to occupy mixed farms, with comparatively low incomes and a culture of growing and preserving much of their own food. They didn't have any money to move away if they wanted to, so they stayed a very tight-knit community.

As a consequence, a lot of traditions other than winemaking remained in the Barossa. We still eat lots of German food — metwurst, fritz, bacon, sausages and other processed meat — made the way it was 160 years ago.

## Traditional preserves

The Barossa Valley is renowned, too, for its root vegetable crops, meats, chickens and pigs. Fruit growing remains important: we have quinces, peaches, pears and plums — much of which is preserved in traditional ways.

All of these foodstuffs are very compatible with wine. And this has encouraged a new generation of people to embrace old Barossa food traditions, while imaginatively building upon them to offer a rich and distinctive local cuisine.

# Matching Wine with Food

## It's the volume of flavour that counts

In matching wine with food, the critical thing, to me, is the volume of flavour — not whether the wine should be red or white. You think about the strength of the flavour in the dish and then select a wine with roughly the equivalent amount of flavour.

For example, Chardonnay or Merlot are interchangeable because they both have a similar volume of flavour. That way, if you're someone who prefers red wine, where you might normally think you should have Chardonnay, you could drink Merlot and still get the same amount of enjoyment — and vice versa.

Try to avoid having food that completely drowns out the wine flavour, or the reverse, where the wine swamps the flavour of an elegant dish.

## To complement or contrast?

Next, consider if you want the flavours to be complementary — because quite often a contrast is better. People often seem to want to serve a sweet wine with a sweet dessert — and you get sugar overload. If you serve something reasonably dry with dessert, the contrast is more attractive because the dryness compensates for the sweetness and vice versa.

If you want to have a sweet wine, then have it with something that's extremely tart, like apple. It's another case of the contrast being more appealing.

## Foiling the oil

Another good contrast is something like Semillon or Semillon Chardonnay with oily food, such as oily fish. Chardonnay on its own is too creamy, but the green grassiness of

Semillon cuts right through that oiliness –
just as a twist of lemon does.

## Cabernet with beef, Shiraz with Italian

It's easy to think, for example, that you've got a
nice piece of steak and you'd better have a big
Shiraz. Well you're not going to taste the steak
– unless you've got a pepper steak. Choose
instead a more elegant wine like Merlot or
Cabernet Sauvignon.

So what do you have with Shiraz? Well,
it's the rule with Italian dishes,
casseroles, or anything with lots
of flavour.

## Wine with curry

Wherever we go in the world
these days we encounter
cuisine that has developed in a
non-vinous environment.
This can be difficult to match
with wine.

The classic one is Indian food. Indians say, ah, yes, but in India, we never drink when we're eating. We don't even drink tea. We drink before and we drink after. It is said that when Indians eat it's very quiet because people drink and talk before — then they eat — and then they drink and talk. The only wine that has a hope with this sort of food is probably something like Grenache because of its perfume.

If food's highly spiced — say with cumin or cardamom — but not hot, then try Riesling or Grenache and Grenache Shiraz. That's because the perfume in these wines matches the perfume in the food, whereas things like Chardonnay and Cabernet just seem to get lost. Shiraz, because of its flavour volume, sometimes works too.

## Riesling and Asian food — made for each other

Japanese and certain Chinese cuisine — Cantonese, for example — is all about fresh flavours. You eat a lot of that food raw and those bright, fresh flavours are just made for wine.

I think one of the best wine and food matches in the world is sashimi and sushi with Riesling. While Chinese food in general goes remarkably well with a number of European wines, I believe that the dry Australian Riesling style is also a remarkable fit.

In Thai food coriander is an important ingredient. Properly handled, you can barely taste it. Even then the perfume overwhelms Chardonnay. But Riesling stands up to it remarkably well.

## Why mouth-puckering reds taste better with protein

When you drink red wine with food rich in protein, such as meat, fish and cheese, there's an instantaneous reaction in your mouth between tannin from the wine and protein from the food. This makes the food texturally more attractive; and the fining effect of the protein on the tannin softens the wine.

So, it's win-win all around. You can demonstrate this to yourself next time you're having a bottle of Cabernet Sauvignon. Make sure you haven't eaten any food for a couple of hours, then have a sip of the wine. It'll be quite mouth puckering. Take your next sip with food and see the difference.

The tip here is that often it's better to taste wine with food to get an idea of how good the wine is — because wine tastings can be somewhat clinical and even misleading for people who don't do it as a profession.

# Brands: What's in a Name?

Apart from geology and climate and all the things that determine the distinctive sorts of wines we make, the use of brands has been one of the keys to Australian export success.

I think that's partly because, more than any other country, Australian winemakers have traditionally produced a range of wine styles — unlike in Europe where people produce Riesling in one area and Cabernet Sauvignon in another.

Winemakers in Australia have been far more catholic in their tastes. That's not just because we don't have restrictive laws telling us where we may and may not plant different varieties — as some European countries do.

## Regional specialities

Perhaps more importantly, it's been in our culture, from the very beginning, to make many different wine styles in single regions. And even as we move towards regional specialities, many wineries — and Jacob's Creek is the perfect example — draw varieties from the most suitable regions in order to offer a wide range of wine styles. Very few Australian winemakers limit their focus to just one or two varieties.

The fact that our winemakers traditionally made a wide range of products, led to the importance of brands within Australia — with the name of a company in many cases becoming the brand. Or, in the case of Jacob's Creek, the name of one of the company vineyards becoming the brand.

"Australian winemakers have traditionally produced a range of wine styles"

"Australian winemakers have made greater use of the strength of brands than anyone else in the world"

# Brands create a trusting relationship

The value of those brands has been strengthened particularly by people drinking wine just for the enjoyment.

If, say, you are a drinker of Jacob's Creek Chardonnay and you decide to try a red wine, there's a fair chance that you'll try one of the Jacob's Creek reds first — and enjoy it too.

I think the best example of this is the success of our Chardonnay Pinot Noir sparkling wine — a product that came into what had traditionally been a market of stand-alone brands, led by Champagne. A big part of its success lay in the brand itself. Imagine that you're buying sparkling wine — and this is usually an occasion thing rather than an everyday thing — and you walk into a store and there's this wall of unfamiliar names. And suddenly you see Jacob's Creek.

The reaction is, I know that. I like their wines. So I'll probably like their sparkling wine.

# Comfortable and confident

If wine brands weren't created by Australia, certainly Australian winemakers have made greater use of the strength of brands than anyone else in the world. And it's worked very much in our favour because if somebody is comfortable with a particular product, it gives them the confidence to try something else under that brand name.

I believe the key to our success is that we have the trust of the people who drink our wines. We've always been very fussy about maintaining the style and improving the quality of Jacob's Creek — and that's the foundation of the relationship we have with our consumers.

# Corks and Closures

If you get a good cork you've got a good bottle of wine, but if you get a bad cork you have an unfortunate bottle of wine. Despite looking and sniffing the cork before putting it into the bottle, there's no way of telling whether it's a good or a bad one.

The only test you can do is a destructive test, and once you've destroyed the cork you no longer have a seal that you can put into a bottle of wine.

**The three problems associated with cork are:**
- cork taint – 2-3% of all corks transmit an unpleasant mouldy characteristic to wine
- cork wood flavour – the cork's woody flavour diminishes the appeal of delicate, fruity wines
- oxidation – the cork lets in air, dulling a wine's aroma and flavour

## Plugging the gap – a new twist

So people have been looking for alternatives, and the solutions have been in two directions. Some people have used look-alike synthetic corks. With very rare exceptions these have failed either because the synthetic material itself imparts a character to the wine, or, more commonly, they let air into the wine and the wine oxidises. Many have also been difficult to remove from the bottle.

A very good alternative, albeit lacking charisma, is the screw cap specifically designed for wine. This was invented in France in the 1950s, tested in Australia in the 1960s and shown to be an outstanding closure.

*The screw cap – the closure of the future.*

But because it didn't have the tradition and ceremony associated with the cork, the foil capsule and the corkscrew, it was not terribly successful. Forty years later consumers, led by Australian and New Zealand winemakers, are eventually coming to accept screw caps on wine.

## Screw caps with a silver lining

Wine screw caps differ from ordinary screw caps even though they might look the same from the outside. If you look inside, the lining is bright silver, being made of pure tin — whereas a screw cap on a bottle of spirits or cordial is usually white, being cellulose.

This thin piece of tin creates a barrier against air. And the tin is separated from the wine by an even thinner layer of plastic. That plastic allows a very small amount of air to penetrate over time into the wine, so that the wine matures under a screw cap almost identically to how it would in a bottle under a good cork.

## As good for reds as for whites

Even a good cork can impart a natural woody flavour to the wine. Now this natural woody flavour of cork doesn't matter in a red wine or a Chardonnay that's been matured in oak — because the oak flavour and the cork flavour are sufficiently similar to disappear into one common flavour.

However, that slightly woody flavour in any wine that has not been matured in oak can actually interfere with your enjoyment of the perfume of the fruit. And that's the primary reason why winemakers in Australia in the mid- to late 1990s started to use screw caps on all of their Rieslings. The same argument was applied in New Zealand with Sauvignon Blanc. Both Riesling and Sauvignon Blanc, being non-oak-matured, were adversely affected by even a very good cork.

increasingly, white wine from all around the world is being bottled under screw cap. And the only apparent reason that this does not apply to red wine to the same extent is more to do with tradition than any other practical reason.

You will increasingly find red wines being bottled under screw caps in the future. New Zealand is providing a good lead in this area, as their Pinot Noir is now almost exclusively bottled under screw cap. Indeed, some Australian and New Zealand makers now use screw caps on all their wines

and in the case of Jacob's Creek, a substantial quantity of St Hugo Coonawarra Cabernet Sauvignon is bottled and sold under screw cap. In fact, you can expect to find all the top end Jacob's Creek wines under screw cap in the not too distant future.

*" Some Australian and New Zealand makers now use screw caps on all their wines "*

# Storing and Serving Wine

There's a big difference between storing a wine in the short term and cellaring it for many years. If you buy a case of wine that you intend to drink over the next few weeks or months, storage conditions are not all that critical.

## Store dark and cool

Certainly the wine does not need to lie on its side. It's perfectly in order to store a wine with a cork in it upright for up to 12 months, unless the wine is very old. And a screw cap wine can be stored upright indefinitely, assuming proper cellaring conditions. But even for such a short time as a couple of months, don't store wine next to a radiator or something that's generating a lot of heat — and keep it away from strong light.

Think very carefully about putting wine away for a long period of time, unless you have somewhere that is dark and cool and stable. By cool I mean around 15 degrees Celsius. Otherwise the chances are when you come to open the bottle of wine you're going to be disappointed. It won't be the fault of the winemaker, but a failure caused by poor storage.

## Wines that age well

If you wish to experiment with ageing Jacob's Creek wines, any of the three Rieslings — but particularly Steingarten — will give fascinating results. Indeed, if stored properly, Steingarten should continue to change in appealing ways for up to 20 years.

Cabernet Sauvignon is another very good variety to put away and mature. Certainly Jacob's Creek Reserve Cabernet Sauvignon and Jacob's Creek St Hugo are wines that will reward you as they age.

Avoid maturing Chardonnay beyond three to four years as it tends to lose its appeal beyond that. And something similar could be said for Shiraz. Beyond eight to ten years it tends to lose the very characteristics — the pepper, spice and plumminess — that make it attractive to drink. It'll still be a lovely, mellow old red — but those distinctive Shiraz notes will be gone.

## Serving wine

When it comes to serving wine, temperature is very important. The concept of room temperature for red wines is great if your room is between 15 and 18 degrees Celsius. If it's warmer or colder, then forget room temperature.

Red wine should be cool but not cold. So 15 to 18, maybe up to 20 degrees. Remember that red wine tends to have more alcohol than white wine and when it becomes warm this alcohol tends to vaporise and produce a very unattractive sensation.

White wines should be served a little cooler, at 10 to 12 degrees. If you over-chill white wine you lose some of the flavour. The exception is sparkling wine, because in order to retain a nice little bubble, you'll need to keep the temperature below 10 degrees.

If you are in an area where it is warm, it's always best to serve too cold rather than too warm. If the wine is too cold it will always warm up – but if it's too warm, it won't cool down. But if it is too cold, and you're desperate, you can always cup your hands around the glass to bring the wine to the right temperature!

## Breathing and decanting

Most wines don't require breathing or decanting. You can generally just remove the cork or screw cap and enjoy them immediately. In the chapter on wine myths, I talk about breathing and why wine generally doesn't need it. But there is a place for decanting wine.

Decanting is a good idea when you have wine that may have a small amount of natural sediment – generally a tartrate deposition – in the bottle. This is most likely to occur in older reds, and can certainly happen in a substantial wine such as Jacob's Creek Centenary Hill Barossa Shiraz.

It's perfectly natural. And in this case you're decanting the wine not to aerate it but to separate the clear wine from the solids. If you just pour from a bottle with solids in it, the constant rocking to and fro as you pour the wine will stir up the deposit. So decanting in that case makes a lot of sense.

## Wine glasses – clear and scrupulously clean

The most important thing is to use clear, scrupulously clean glasses. Despite what people say, it's generally not necessary to avoid using detergent. All it takes is a good rinse to remove residual detergent scents after washing. It's also important not to clean glasses in water that's been used for washing dishes and pans as they pick up food flavours.

# Think tulips not fishbowls

To get the most out of your wine, try to use tulip-shaped glasses as these tend to concentrate the aromas. Stems are important, too. A stem prevents the warmth of your hand being transferred to the wine — and it means no greasy fingerprints on the bowl to detract from the appearance of the wine.

There's a tendency for people all over the world now to serve wines in enormous, balloon-shaped glasses. This is quite ridiculous. You want the surface of the wine to be large enough to allow some air to get to it. But you don't need a fishbowl to achieve this.

At a dinner party it's ideal to have a separate glass for each wine. But the glasses can be of the same shape. There's no need to have different-shaped glasses for red and white wine.

In some cases it's quite okay to use the same glass for more than one wine, especially for similar wine styles. But you wouldn't want to pour dry wine into a glass from which you'd previously drunk sweet wine. And while red wine can follow white in one glass, quite clearly it can't be the other way around.

*“Try to use tulip-shaped glasses as these tend to concentrate the aromas”*

# Wine Awards

Wine Awards from recognised and reputable organisations are of great value to wine drinkers as a guide to quality. An award is an indication — from an independent group of people — that a particular bottle of wine compared very favourably not only against its competitors but also against the standards that the judges carry around in their heads.

Wine competitions are also of great value to winemakers because they provide an opportunity to compare their skills with their peers from within the same country or around the world. As in any form of exhibition, wine shows and competitions encourage winemakers to improve the attractiveness and quality of their product.

## There are gold discs and Gold Medals

The fact that a gold disc appears on a bottle may mean nothing more than that the wine was founded in such and such a year. Make sure that the medal actually relates to a specific wine show and that it records the class and the description of the class that the wine was exhibited in.

You can be reassured by awards from reputable shows. Awards from Australian State capital city wine shows — Sydney, Melbourne, Canberra, Adelaide, Hobart, Brisbane and Perth — are a very good indication of quality.

## Australia's wine shows

The reason that Australian winemakers and consumers put so much confidence in our wine shows is that they are run by independent organisations, not the industry. These are principally State-based agricultural societies. And the events that they conduct are broad-based agricultural shows — of which wine is just one component — aimed at improving the breed.

Judges at Australian wine shows never see a bottle or a label — just glasses of wine poured by independent stewards. The judges are drawn largely from the winemaking fraternity — those people recognised as having particularly good palates. But they are balanced by other people who have skills in assessing and commenting on wine — principally from the restaurant and retail trades, and wine media.

## International judges

With the growth of Australian wine exports most Australian wine shows now include international judges on their panels to broaden the judging perspective. And to reassure consumers that wine show medals on bottles are genuine, the shows have rigorous auditing procedures in place.

# Reading the Label

## What are the most important things to look for on a wine label?

The first thing to look for is the brand or the name of the winemaker, because that brand or person's reputation is going to tell you a lot about the wine. That's the first clue as to quality.

You may then have in mind a particular variety or style. So the label will then tell you whether it's a single variety or a blend — bearing in mind that in many cases the blend may well be more attractive than a single variety.

Next you look at the vintage — bearing in mind that in a bottle of wine from Australia the vintage does not have the significance that it might have in northern Europe, due to our more even climate.

The label will also tell you the source of the grapes that went into the wine. And again this may be fruit from a single area or it might be a blend from a range of areas. While single regions are not necessarily better than blends of regions, it's still important that the grapes came from an area or areas suited to the variety or varieties.

"First impressions are important: read the label if you want to get to know a wine"

# Judging Wine by Price

## Can you judge a wine by its price?

The truth is that this is not an easy question to answer. Price is one indication of quality. But be very careful because pricing can be used where something's very scarce, in which case price reflects that scarcity. This probably means that the wine's very good — but maybe not as good as the price might suggest.

Some people believe that by paying a really high price they're getting a really good bottle of wine. What you have to do if you buy a really expensive bottle of wine is to be brutally honest in your assessment of it. Say, yes, I am enjoying this, irrespective of the price. Or, if you're not enjoying it, say so. The chances are the price is wrong and not you.

## How do I trade up for a special occasion?

If you want to try something a little better than what you usually drink — whether it's because you're out to impress someone or just want to enjoy the experience — price is a pretty good guide within a single brand range like Jacob's Creek.

For example, if you compared our Riesling or Shiraz to the Reserve Riesling or Reserve Shiraz you'd have no difficulty discerning — and enjoying — the extra flavour and complexity you get for your money.

You could then take another step up in price to Steingarten Riesling or Centenary Hill Shiraz and experience wine of an altogether greater dimension — but in the context of Jacob's Creek's elegance and drinkability.

# Assessing Wine

### How do I assess a wine?

The only way you can assess wine is in a clear, clean glass. The colour tells you an awful lot about the wine. With white wine you would be looking for tinges of green, irrespective of its age. With the exception of a couple of varieties that inherently don't have green, that green tinge is a very good indication of how the fruit was picked, how the wine was made and how it's been warehoused and cared for.

Similarly with red, in a wine of up to 4-5 years old you would be expecting to see some purple hues and in an older wine some crimson. But in all cases if you start to see browns be very careful unless the wine is very old, in which case some browning in red is to be expected.

The nose is going to tell you all about the flavour of the wine and its varietal characteristics. You are looking for things that are fresh. The first thing you should smell is the fruit, or a combination that is all about the fruit.

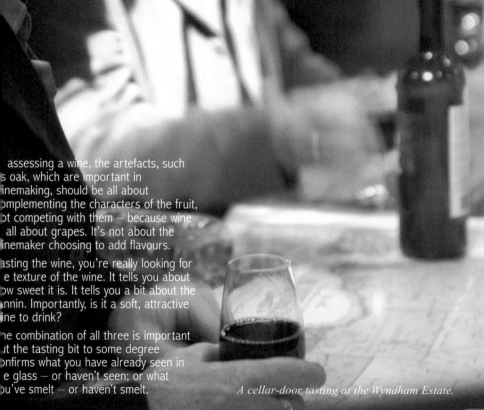

assessing a wine, the artefacts, such
s oak, which are important in
inemaking, should be all about
omplementing the characters of the fruit,
ot competing with them — because wine
all about grapes. It's not about the
inemaker choosing to add flavours.

asting the wine, you're really looking for
e texture of the wine. It tells you about
ow sweet it is. It tells you a bit about the
nnin. Importantly, is it a soft, attractive
ine to drink?

he combination of all three is important
ut the tasting bit to some degree
onfirms what you have already seen in
e glass — or haven't seen; or what
ou've smelt — or haven't smelt.

*A cellar-door tasting at the Wyndham Estate.*

# Talking About Vintages

### Does the vintage matter?

Yes, vintage does have a bearing on quality and some years are better than others. But we are very fortunate that our seasonal variations in Australia are generally nowhere near as great as in parts of Europe. And to be honest about it, we rarely have a very bad year. The last was in 1983.

We don't try to hide these vintage differences. In good years we play them up, particularly in the Jacob's Creek Reserve and Heritage ranges. But right at the top end there are years when we might say, for one style or variety, the year isn't good enough to make and bottle that wine.

However, generally speaking, because we can blend from different regions across Australia, we tend to get more evenness between vintages than our counterparts in mos parts of the world.

# Is older better?

Age cannot improve wine. Wine is at its best when it's hanging as a bunch of grapes on the vine. Everything we do thereafter tends to detract from the quality of that fruit. The skill of the winemaker is to minimise the damage done to the fruit in getting it into a bottle.

If you put away a bottle of ordinary wine for ten years, when you open it up you have a ten-year-old bottle of ordinary wine.

If you put away a very good bottle of wine for ten years, it's not going to get better. But the reason people like to drink 10- or 15-year-old bottles of Riesling or Cabernet Sauvignon is because the changes that have taken place make the wine very interesting.

In any event 99% of us have nowhere suitable to store a bottle of wine. And that's not just speaking as an Australian from a very hot country. Even for people living in the cooler UK, it's still difficult to ensure a stable temperature – because of central heating, air conditioning and seasonal variations.

So, if you do want to put a bottle of wine away for a 21st birthday or whatever, you need to have ideal storage conditions – a stable 14 to 18 degrees Celsius – or else recognise that you're putting it away more for the ceremony than the enjoyment.

# Debunking Wine Myths

"*Does wine **really** need to breathe?*"

## Myth: Wine needs to breathe

The concept of pulling the cork out hours before drinking goes back many, many decades to a time when winemakers did not have the resources that they have today. And quite frequently the process of fermentation would leave some unattractive volatile characteristics. The reason for pulling the cork out — or for that matter decanting the wine — was to allow these unattractive odours to dissipate.

Of course, as you're losing the unattractive odours you are also losing some of the attractive ones. So if you have a very good bottle of wine and you pull the cork and let it breathe, all you're doing is diminishing your pleasure, because these lovely characteristics disappear into the ether.

Certain wines that have been bottle aged can benefit from breathing. But unless you have actually tasted that wine before and discovered that it requires breathing, don't take the risk — because nine times out of ten, the wine's going to be more attractive if you pull the cork immediately before consumption.

If you decide that a wine does need a bit of breathing, you can generally aerate it enough by pouring it into your glass and swirling it around.

## Myth: Riesling is sweet

No wine varietal is inherently sweet or dry. The winemaker starts with grape juice containing a certain amount of natural grape sugar in it. Fermentation converts this sugar to alcohol. It's then the winemaker's choice whether or not to convert all of the sugar to alcohol.

Sometimes Australian winemakers leave a small amount of what we call residual sugar in white wines — and this is true of many Rieslings — to temper the acidity. This is generally a small amount and most Australian Rieslings, unless the label says otherwise, will be dry. The three Rieslings in the Jacob's Creek range are all dry.

## Myth: Screw caps are only for drink-now wines

Another myth is that the modern-day use of screw caps is fine for wines that are to be drunk immediately but for wines you want to cellar for some time the screw caps are such an effective seal that the wine won't mature.

This is incorrect because 50% of maturation characteristics do not require the presence of oxygen. However, the 50% that do, receive sufficient oxygen through the thin plastic film in a screw cap that separates the tin seal from the wine.

## Myth: You must rotate bottles of wine maturing in your cellar

I'm not sure where this myth came from, but it's amazing how many people believe in it. In fact, quite the reverse is true. The less the wine is disturbed, the better it is going to be. Certainly there is no way in the world that rotating it is going to improve it.

*Certain white wines can mature just as attractively and for just as long as reds*

"If you intend to keep the wine for longer than 12 months then the bottle should lie on its side to keep the cork moist and airtight"

## Myth: You can only cellar red wines

The thing that determines the maturation value of a wine is how it's going to change over time. Certain white wines can mature just as attractively and for just as long as any red wine will. Australian Riesling — including Jacob's Creek Riesling, Reserve Riesling and Steingarten Riesling — all develop attractive flavours with bottle age, the latter two for a decade or more given ideal cellaring conditions.

## Myth: Wine sealed with a cork must lie on its side

This is only true if you are not planning to drink the wine within 6-12 months of purchase. If you intend to keep the wine for longer than 12 months then the bottle should lie on its side to keep the cork moist and airtight.

## Myth: Red wine should be served at room temperature

Red wine should be served at 15 to 20 degrees Celsius. Room temperature is a dangerous expression for the simple reason that rooms vary in temperature whether it's through climatic differences (Glasgow versus Morocco, for example), seasonal differences, and presence or absence of sunlight, heaters and air conditioners.

# Our Wines

Our winemaking philosophy starts with our belief that eight or nine of every ten bottles of Jacob's Creek are drunk around food. It's therefore very important that we make a style of wine that sits comfortably with food.

Now the majority of people having a glass of wine aren't consciously thinking about the wine. They're not thinking about which side of the hill it came from, perhaps not even of the variety.

If they enjoy the wine, then they remember it. And this is very important to us. What is it, then, that makes wines that go well with food? To me it's all about freshness and elegance — two key characteristics of Jacob's Creek.

## Grape flavours

Freshness first: it's very important that the grape flavours come through. If it's Riesling, it actually has to taste like Riesling. If it's Cabernet Sauvignon, you want the green leaf and the cassis to come through and you don't want it be overly complicated with oak and other flavours.

The elegant bit's very important because it's easy for Australian wines to be overwhelming with food. Shiraz is a classic example – we in Australia make these wonderful Shirazes but when do you drink them?

I often describe Jacob's Creek as being a bit like a hybrid between Australia and Europe. I think the Europeans, over 2000 years, worked out that the wines people actually liked with food were the more elegant ones. However, if you put Jacob's Creek into a European line-up, it appears very Australian. It bears little resemblance to Europe. But if you put it in a line-up with Australian wines you can actually taste some of those European tendencies on the palate.

## Flavour without heaviness

We are sometimes criticised at tastings for making wines that are too light. But this is not the way people drink wine. They don't line up four glasses of Australian Chardonnay with whatever they're eating. They have a glass of this one or that one. What we're doing is producing something that works very well in that dining situation.

So we've always believed in elegance. Now you might call it lightness. But to me lightness is all about emptiness and lacking. These wines aren't lacking anything; they're just not overpowering.

We reckon there's a link through the sparkling wines, the white wines and the red wines with the same characteristics of freshness and elegance coming through. It's almost an oxymoron talking about elegant Shiraz. But if you look at Jacob's Creek Shiraz in the context of a lot of other Australian Shiraz, it certainly comes through as being a lighter, more elegant style.

That elegance is more a palate function than a fruit function. You can still have lots to smell and taste but at the same time you don't have to have a big, overwhelming palate. And it's that palate sensation that I think all too easily interferes with food.

## Regional fruit selection and attentive winemaking

If we're right about the style — and there's plenty of evidence to show that it's well loved — then the question is how do you achieve it?  It's not a matter of putting a water hose in to dilute things back.

That's where it comes back to selecting regions — or blends of regions, blends of varieties if need be, to capture the freshness and elegance we desire. It's the combination of fruit selection and attentive but not intrusive winemaking that makes Jacob's Creek what it is.

## The style evolves gradually

It's important for Jacob's Creek wines to remain contemporary — what people want to drink today. That's why the wines of ten years ago is not the style that people expect today.

One good example would be the move away from excessive artefacts in winemaking. Fifteen years ago, we would have had a lot more obvious oak. It would have had a lot more malolactic characters — flavours from fermentation that were competing with the fruit — than today when all those artefacts are at a complementary level.

As I travel around the world I listen to what people are saying and observe what's happening. Yet there aren't enormous differences between trends in North America, the UK, Scandinavia, Australia and many parts of Asia. There seems to be a fairly common approach to drinking wine all around the world.

**Serving temperature:**

15-18 degrees Celsius.

**Colour:**

Medium-depth crimson red.

**Smells of:**

Plum and blackberry with spicy notes plus hints of cassis, complemented by restrained sweet vanilla oak.

**Tastes of:**

Fresh red berries and lightly toasted oak creating an attractive sweet mid-palate, with balanced tannins forming a soft persistent finish.

**Goes with:**

Richly flavoured Italian dishes, casseroles, lamb or savoury snacks.

# Shiraz Cabernet

This blend combines the soft, plummy generosity of Shiraz with the slightly firmer structure of Cabernet Sauvignon. It's a versatile wine suited to all sorts of food from richly flavoured Italian dishes to casseroles, lamb or savoury nibbles. The warming effect of Shiraz makes it a good cool-weather wine.

# Cabernet Sauvignon

Cabernet's mix of dark berries, leafiness and fairly firm tannin structure makes it a great match for high-protein dishes, especially a prime cut of steak. That's because the protein in the food fines — or softens — the grippy tannins in the wine, and the tannins temper the proteins. Sounds technical, but it works. Because Cabernet Sauvignon produces a cooling effect, it's an excellent warm-weather red.

**Serving temperature:**

15-18 degrees Celsius.

**Colour:**

Deep and vibrant crimson red.

**Smells of:**

Intense varietal aromas of cassis, a hint of leaf and subtle oak-influenced characters of cedar and vanilla.

**Tastes of:**

Concentrated varietal fruit flavours of blackcurrant and dark berries with cinnamon and spice. A structural wine revealing a full- to medium-weight palate with elegant yet persistent fine tannins and a long finish.

**Goes with:**

Steak and other meat dishes.

### Serving temperature:

18 degrees Celsius in cold weather; can also be lightly chilled in summer.

### Colour:

Full-depth crimson with purple hues indicating freshness.

### Smells of:

Fresh berry fruit, with violets, dark berries and black pepper.

### Tastes of:

Rich, ripe blackberry, blood-plum and spice with a full, fleshy mid-palate. Outstanding depth of fruit flavour supported by subtle coffee-like oak notes and fine velvety tannins.

### Goes with:

Chicken, pork and rich winter stews.

# Shiraz

This one expresses the very appealing fresh berry fruits, black pepper and spice of the variety. It also has characteristic soft, velvety tannin, making it very appealing to sip even without food. For food matches, think of chicken, pork or rich winter stews.

Although it works best in cool weather, it'll also suit summer meals. Just chill it lightly in the fridge — but not too long.

# Merlot

Merlot's often blended with Cabernet Sauvignon, but here it stands on its own as a medium-bodied wine delivering an attractive plump, juicy palate with persistent soft tannins. The generous fruit and soft tannins make it a good match with pasta, pizza and cheese. Or, if you're feeling a little daring, it works well with full-flavoured fish such as salmon or herring.

### Serving temperature:
15-18 degrees Celsius.

### Colour:
Mid-crimson red with a purple hue.

### Smells of:
Concentrated berry fruits with distinctive mulberry aromas, also showing accents of cherry and black olive, with restrained vanilla and cedar notes playing a supporting role.

### Tastes of:
Fresh varietal fruit and sweet vanilla oak flavours. A well-rounded, luscious mid-palate precedes a soft yet persistent finish built on supple tannins.

### Goes with:
Pasta, pizza and cheese; tuna or salmon steak.

**Serving temperature:**

18 degrees Celsius in cool weather; 14-15 degrees in summer.

**Colour:**

Vibrant medium crimson.

**Smells of:**

Fresh, juicy raspberry and cherry fruit, with hints of rose petal, white pepper and spice.

**Tastes of:**

Lively and fruit-driven, with cherry syrup and berry confection notes; soft and fleshy structure, with surprisingly persistent length of flavour to a clean finish.

**Goes with:**

Delicious on its own on a warm summer's day, or as a partner for Asian cuisine, including curry.

# Grenache Shiraz

In this blend Shiraz plays a supporting role to the perfumed, seductive raspberry and cherry high notes of Grenache. It's a classic combination, marked by very bright and refreshing fruit flavours and very fine, silky tannins. The perfume helps it to match spicy Asian food and it has some chance with curry, too. In cool weather serve it at around 18 degrees Celsius. At a summer lunch, you could probably bring that down to 14 or 15 degrees.

# Semillon Sauvignon Blanc

Light and zesty refreshment probably
best sums up this extremely versatile blend. It's light
enough as a refresher in its own right.
But the zesty, lemon character
acts as a great foil to the
oiliness of fish. And it works just
as well with a bowl of steaming
mussels or a crisp and crunchy
summer salad.

**Serving temperature:**
Serve well chilled.

**Colour:**
Vibrant straw green.

**Smells of:**
Fresh lemon and ripe tropical
characters with added
complexity contributed by
grassy notes.

**Tastes of:**
Ripe Semillon provides
lemony flavours and a
focused structure while
Sauvignon Blanc contributes
fresh gooseberry and
tropical fruit, with a crisp
grassy finish.

**Goes with:**
Oily fish, mussels, light
salads.

**Serving temperature:**

Serve chilled, but less so in cooler weather.

**Colour:**

Vibrant straw with flecks of brilliant green.

**Smells of:**

Fresh lemon grass and citrus melon.

**Tastes of:**

Soft, clean, and lemony with balanced, lively and refreshing acidity on the finish.

**Goes with:**

Chicken, oily fish, salads.

# Semillon Chardonnay

This is a halfway house between the opulence of Chardonnay and the lemony austerity of Semillon. It's light and fresh enough to drink on its own. It's flavoursome enough to match chicken. It's also zesty enough to cut through the oiliness of fish. Works equally well in cool and warm conditions.

# Riesling

Jacob's Creek Riesling shows the true breeding of this great variety, sourced from the right growing regions. It's a delicate, dry style featuring intense lemon and lime flavours and mineral acidity. It's glorious with sushi, sashimi and grilled, delicate fish. It goes well with Asian food in general but is also good on its own or with finger food. It takes on appealing honeyed flavours with bottle age.

**Serving temperature:**
Serve moderately chilled.

**Colour:**
Vibrant straw with green hues.

**Smells of:**
Fresh lemons and limes with underlying ripe tropical fruit notes.

**Tastes of:**
Fruit-driven lively lemons and limes. Soft and flavoursome with natural mineral acidity creating balance and length of flavour.

**Goes with:**
Sushi, sashimi, grilled fish, most Asian food.

**Serving temperature:**

Serve moderately chilled.

**Colour:**

Medium straw yellow with deep green hues.

**Smells of:**

Intense white peach and melon fruit with a background of nutty oak and buttery complexity.

**Tastes of:**

Intense peach melon fruit flavours with complex nutty oak and creamy characters. The texture is soft and silky and balanced by a fresh acid finish.

**Goes with:**

Chicken, pasta dishes, full-flavoured seafood such as lobster.

# Chardonnay

The thumbprint of all the Jacob's Creek Chardonnays is their generous but refined peach and melon flavours, supplemented by subtle oak characters. The soft texture and full flavour makes this wine well suited to chicken and pasta dishes, stronger seafood like lobster and even, if the fancy takes you, a simple char-grilled steak. Want a white in winter? Chardonnay's the go as it's rich, full and warming.

# Shiraz Rosé

The attractive fresh berry aromas and soft spicy flavours reflect the cool-climate Shiraz used in this wine's making. It has great vibrancy and freshness to go with the spicy, berry flavours, making it an all-rounder. For this reason it suits a really wide range of foods, especially in a casual environment — like pizza on the lap watching cricket, at a picnic or as an after-work refresher.

**Serving temperature:**

Serve lightly chilled.

**Colour:**

Vibrant salmon pink.

**Smells of:**

Fresh and spicy raspberry fruit with a subtle sweet confection background.

**Tastes of:**

Soft, sweet raspberry-spice fruit flavours harmoniously balanced with lively acidity on the finish.

**Goes with:**

Almost everything; think pizza, picnics, and apéritif.

# The Reserve Range

*The Reserves are single varieties drawn from even more highly specialised regions than the standard blends*

# Reserve Shiraz

When we make wine for the Reserve range it's not a just matter of making a better Chardonnay, Riesling, Shiraz or Cabernet Sauvignon. It is very much a matter of making a better varietal wine that is completely faithful to the Jacob's Creek style.

This is pure, classic Shiraz, with layers and layers of beautiful, spicy, plummy fruit flavours meshed with soft, satisfying tannins. Bold but velvety tannins provide the perfect backbone for expression of concentrated, spicy Shiraz flavours. The wine has great length of flavour, with complex notes of liquorice, coffee and blackberry evident. It's best served with equally generously flavoured food like game, beef and veal casseroles or dishes involving earthy mushroom sauces — think winter, think rich, think warm.

**Serving temperature:**
15-18 degrees Celsius.

**Colour:**
Vibrant crimson with purple highlights.

**Smells of:**
Attractive wild blackberry, sweet spices and violets with subtle mocha-like oak notes.

**Tastes of:**
Intense dark berry fruit flavours, with layers of anise and spice. Full-bodied with strong palate presence and length.

**Goes with:**
Casseroles of game, beef or veal.

**Serving temperature:**

15-18 degrees Celsius.

**Colour:**

Full-depth crimson ruby.

**Smells of:**

Ripe cassis and blackberry fruit with hints of crushed herbs and dark chocolate underpinned with subtle cedar oak notes.

**Tastes of:**

Intensely varietal dark forest fruits with violets, vine-leaf and black olive nuances.

**Goes with:**

Beef or lamb.

# Reserve Cabernet Sauvignon

There's an austerity about Cabernet as the tannins take on a more central role than they do in Shiraz — creating a focus on the structure of the wine. But beneath that firmness, good Cabernet has a subtle depth of berry, leafy and black-olive fruit flavour. Well-integrated spicy oak adds palate weight and flavour complexity. Finely textured tannins give the wine a balanced structure and complement the persistent fruit flavours. The combination is just wonderful and makes Jacob's Creek Reserve a wine to savour with fine cuts of beef or lamb.

Reserve wines are great value for money, and we achieve this by careful attention to regional fruit selection. ”

**Serving temperature:**

Serve moderately chilled.

**Colour:**

Vibrant straw colour with a hint of green.

**Smells of:**

Fresh and attractive passionfruit and tropical-fruit notes with subtle hints of green gooseberry.

**Tastes of:**

Delicious tropical fruit flavours backed by a lively acidity that carries through to a fruity and refreshingly dry finish.

**Goes with:**

A delicious refresher on its own, or suits light, fresh food such as salad, asparagus or a bowl of mussels.

# Reserve Sauvignon Blanc

Jacob's Creek Sauvignon Blanc captures the racy, zesty passionfruit and tropical-fruit character of this distinctive variety. Though intensely fruity, the wine has lightness and a delicate, bracing acidity. This combination of dazzling fruit and lively acidity makes Reserve Sauvignon Blanc a great warm-weather tipple and friendly company over summer lunches and twilight dinners.

# Reserve Riesling

Our Reserve Riesling brings together fruit from Australia's leading Riesling growing regions — the Eden, Clare and Barossa Valleys. This wine has freshness, intensity of lime flavour and drying, delicate mineral acidity, with a clean, chalky finish. This gives it enormous appeal as a lightly chilled apéritif and as a wine to serve with delicate seafood and salads. Like all dry Rieslings it also suits most Asian cuisine.

**Serving temperature:**

Lightly chilled.

**Colour:**

Vibrant green.

**Smells of:**

Fresh, rich citrus lime and floral spice.

**Tastes of:**

Fruit-driven with intense tropical lime and lemon sherbet. Persistent minerally acid provides freshness and length, completed by a clean, chalky finish.

**Goes with:**

Seafood, salads, Asian cuisine; or as an apéritif.

**Serving temperature:**

Lightly chilled.

**Colour:**

Medium straw yellow with deep, vibrant green hues.

**Smells of:**

Intense white peach and melon fruit with a background of nutty oak and buttery complexity.

**Tastes of:**

Fresh, long, white peach, melon and citrus fruit flavours that marry well with the nutty, cedar oak flavours. The texture is soft and creamy and balanced by a fresh acid finish.

**Goes with:**

Rich, non-oily dishes such as chicken, veal and lobster.

# Reserve Chardonnay

This wine captures the intense melon and peach flavours of Chardonnay grown in the cooler parts of South Australia. With this intensity of fruit the wine easily carries the complexities introduced through fermentation and maturation in French oak barrels. This process introduces subtle, buttery and nutty oak flavours and a rich texture, with a fresh acid finish. Although there's a great volume of flavour, the wine is vibrant, fresh and beautifully balanced. It's therefore best served lightly chilled with quite rich but not oily dishes. Chicken, veal and fresh lobster are all excellent choices.

# Reserve Chardonnay Pinot Noir

A key component of this Reserve sparkling wine comes from Tasmania, our southernmost growing region. Serve moderately chilled as an apéritif, with summer lunches, on the boat, or whenever there's reason to celebrate.

**Serving temperature:**

Chilled.

**Colour:**

Vibrant mid-straw green with a fine gas.

**Smells of:**

The refreshing lemon citrus aroma of Chardonnay in harmony with the red berry characters of Pinot Noir. Creamy yeast complexity supports the fruit aromas.

**Tastes of:**

Generous cool-climate citrus flavours with creamy yeast characters providing richness, structure and length. The wine finishes crisp and dry, with a deliciously lingering nutty aftertaste.

**Goes with:**

Light lunches; or as an apéritif, or for a special occasion.

# The Sparkling Range

*"Sparkling wines should have a balance of delicacy and richness, which is only achievable using some grapes from cooler vineyards"*

The production of sparkling wines with that rare combination of richness and delicacy requires fruit grown in a very cool climate. That's because grapes ripened in cool conditions retain fresh acidity and develop delicate fruit flavours before the sugar levels — and therefore potential alcohol — become too high.

**Serving temperature:**

Chilled.

**Colour:**

Mid-straw green with a fine and persistent mousse.

**Smells of:**

The citrus and toasted cashew nut flavours of Chardonnay and the fresh, attractive bread crust characters of Pinot Noir.

**Tastes of:**

Elegant fruit flavours enhanced with creamy yeast providing depth and flavour. The wine finishes soft, crisp and clean.

**Goes with:**

Dessert; or as an apéritif or party wine.

# Chardonnay Pinot Noir Brut Cuvée

Our aim with this wine is to capture the crisp, elegant fruit flavours of Chardonnay and Pinot Noir, subtly enhanced by maturation on yeast lees, which produces a creamy, nutty character. This gives the wine a delightful freshness and leaves a lovely sense of cleanliness. It's best served chilled and creates its own occasion. It goes as well with dessert as it does as an apéritif or party starter.

### Hold on to your cork

Did you know that pressure inside a bottle of sparkling wine is about the same as in a bus tyre? That explains why a cork escapes at such velocity — and why you should **never** let one go.

### White wine from red grapes

How do we make clear sparkling wine from red Pinot Noir grapes? The trick is to separate the juice from the skin quickly and without applying too much pressure to the skins. This is because the flesh and juice are clear and all the colour pigments are in the skins.

# Sparkling Rosé

This is a sparkling wine in which the red grapes of the Pinot Noir component have been allowed to deliver a lovely pink blush of colour. The Pinot also gives an appealing fresh strawberry character that helps to distinguish the style from clear sparkling wines. It's a party time, outdoors, warm weather, picnicky sort of wine with seriously good fresh flavours.

### Serving temperature:

Well chilled.

### Colour:

Soft pink colour with a fine and persistent mousse.

### Smells of:

The lemon citrus aromas of Chardonnay and the fresh strawberry and redcurrant characters of Pinot Noir.

### Tastes of:

Generous red berry and citrus fruit flavours with creamy yeast providing depth and flavour. The wine finishes soft and round, with lingering berry flavours.

### Goes with:

Summer picnics and parties, and fruit desserts.

# The Heritage Range

*"Each of our Heritage wines is a classic Australian style"*

The Heritage Range from Jacob's Creek is a fitting tribute to the brand's rich history, showcasing outstanding examples of benchmark regional varietal Australian wines. Centenary Hill Shiraz, Steingarten Riesling, Reeves Point Chardonnay and St Hugo Cabernet Sauvignon are examples of classic Australian styles.

Centenary Hill Shiraz comes from vineyards along Jacob's Creek and expresses the particular rich but elegant character of our cooler end of the Barossa.

Steingarten Riesling – from the Steingarten and neighbouring vineyards in the eastern hills in Jacob's Creek catchment – rates as one of the finest examples of this distinguished regional style.

Reeves Point Chardonnay expresses the unique, elegant melon and peach characters of the best Chardonnay from cool Padthaway – some 400km south of Jacob's Creek.

Another 100km south, in Coonawarra, Cabernet Sauvignon is the local speciality. This is the source of the powerful, refined Jacob's Creek St Hugo Cabernet Sauvignon.

**Serving temperature:**

15-18 degrees Celsius.

**Colour:**

Deep ruby red.

**Smells of:**

Intense chocolate, ground spice and stewed plum with nuances of black pepper, eucalyptus and leather, highlighted by integrated mocha oak.

**Tastes of:**

Dense, youthful, rich and structured in its intense concentration, balanced by savoury fruit flavours and moderately firm tannin finish with excellent length of flavour.

**Goes with:**

Casseroles of game, beef or veal.

# Centenary Hill Barossa Valley Shiraz

A fine example of a classic full-bodied Barossa Shiraz from an outstanding vintage that, while just beginning to offer excellent drinking now, will continue to develop in pleasant ways for many years, assuming good cellaring. It's sourced from vineyards along Jacob's Creek in the southern Barossa. It's a cool part of the Barossa and this adds distinctive savoury no and some elegance to the structure. This wine's too go to rush. Sip and savour is the order of the day. Enjoy every drop.

## Cool Creek

Why is it cooler at Jacob's Creek than in other parts of the Barossa? Well, it's towards the southern end, so that's an influence. And the vineyards also benefit from cool night air flowing down Jacob's Creek from the hills to the east.

# St Hugo Coonawarra Cabernet Sauvignon

We source St Hugo from Coonawarra in the far south of South Australia. The area's part of a great limestone formation bounded to the south and west by the Southern Ocean. Coonawarra's shallow, red *terra rossa* soils, overlying the limestone, have proven to be one of the very best places in the world to grow Cabernet. St Hugo reflects this provenance, delivering great power with elegance – hallmarks of the best examples of the variety. This wine may be cellared for a decade or more.

**Serving temperature:**

15-18 degrees Celsius.

**Colour:**

Deep vibrant red with crimson highlights.

**Smells of:**

Intense blackcurrant, mint and crushed violets supported by cedar and dark chocolate gained from barrel fermentation and maturation in French oak.

**Tastes of:**

Concentrated blackcurrants and blackberries intertwined with firm youthful tannins and oak-derived spiciness. The palate has excellent fruit richness balanced by refreshing acidity and impressive fine-grained tannin structure. The length is satisfying with a touch of savouriness.

**Goes with:**

Steak and other meat dishes.

**Serving temperature:**

Lightly chilled.

**Colour:**

Bright pale-straw yellow with vibrant green hue.

**Smells of:**

Fragrant, delicate lemon blossom with floral overtones

**Tastes of:**

Lemony citrus with a hint of limes. These flavours are long but show great finesse and are supported by a tight minerally acid structure and refreshing crisp finish.

**Goes with:**

Seafood, salads, Asian cuisine; or as an apéritif.

### Stay high, keep cool

The few kilometres that separate Steingarten Vineyard from Jacob's Creek mean an extra few hundred metres elevation. This creates the cooler conditions that bring out the best flavours in Riesling.

# Steingarten Barossa Riesling

Steingarten is the name of a vineyard planted in 1962 by the Gramp family on a stony, elevated slope a few kilometres east of Jacob's Creek and on the same catchment. The area, in general, produces some of Australia's finest Rieslings, and Steingarten Vineyard gives its name and contributes some of the fruit to this classic wine. It's a superb aromatic style with potential to cellar for up to 20 years. Serve only lightly chilled in order to enjoy the full range of aromas and flavours.

# Reeves Point Chardonnay

Reeves Point Chardonnay is an outstanding example of a complex, cool-climate Australian Chardonnay. Great intensity of varietal flavour, a seamless and creamy texture and focused palate structure are the key features of this wine, which can be enjoyed now, but will reward careful cellaring. The wine has an excellent acid balance that adds freshness and will ensure graceful bottle ageing.

## Why Reeves Point?

In his migration from Bavaria to South Australia, Johann Gramp landed and stayed at Reeves Point on Kangaroo Island, just south of Adelaide, for a few months before crossing to the mainland and settling at Jacob's Creek.

### Serving temperature:
Lightly chilled.

### Colour:
Pale straw with vibrant green hues.

### Smells of:
Fresh citrus, melon and white peach fruit in harmony with nutty, vanilla French oak overtones.

### Tastes of:
Concentrated melon, citrus and stonefruit complemented by soft, creamy yeast and delicate nutty oak nuances. This wine has an excellent structure with great length of flavours that are complex, yet fresh.

### Goes with:
Rich, non-oily dishes such as chicken, veal and lobster.

# Our Icon Wine

## One to put down

Jacob's Creek Johann Shiraz Cabernet has been bottle matured at the winery, so it is still fresh yet well integrated, and will delight those who choose to drink it now. On the other hand, carefully cellaring this wine for the next 5-10 years will enable further development and integration of its ripe and intense fruit flavours.

# Johann Shiraz Cabernet

Johann is the flagship of the Jacob's Creek range and is a blend of Shiraz from Jacob's Creek in the Barossa and Cabernet Sauvignon from Coonawarra, almost 400km to the south. Structure and elegance is achieved by carefully marrying Shiraz with selected parcels of Cabernet Sauvignon, each fermented separately to give greater complexity to the blend. The integrated flavours of spice, black pepper, cassis and red berry are achieved through carefully blending only the best Shiraz and Cabernet Sauvignon grapes. Johann represents the pinnacle of our winemaking expertise and is available in extremely limited quantities.

**Serving temperature:**

15-18 degrees Celsius.

**Colour:**

Deep ruby crimson.

**Smells of:**

Integrated spices and black pepper with luscious juicy cassis and red berry. Developed aniseed and liquorice notes along with integrated savoury oak give this wine complexity and richness.

**Tastes of:**

This wine shows enormous depth of fruit, with concentrated ripe blackcurrant and juicy blueberry flavours seamlessly integrated with savoury, charry oak. Well-structured tannins give it elegance and finesse while still providing a balance with the wine's intense ripe fruit characters

**Goes with:**

Lamb or richly flavoured Italian dishes.

# Index